Günter Gerngross • Herbert Puchta

PLAYWAY 3

PUPIL'S BOOK

Helbling

Unit
1 Back to school

1 Listen and speak.

1 CD 1/2

2 Listen and fill in the numbers.

3 Test your partner.

2 CD 1/3

4 Listen and mime. Then listen and point.

Party time

5 Listen and fill in the numbers.

6 Listen and point. Sing the song.

Oh, what a lovely morning

You're in bed,
and you wake up.
You check your watch.
It's time to get up!

Oh, what a lovely morning,
it's time to go to school.
Oh, what a lovely morning,
school is so cool!
School is so cool!

Wash your face,
put on your clothes.
Have a glass of milk.
Take your bag, and off you go!

Oh, what a lovely morning,
it's time to go to school.
Oh, what a lovely morning,
school is so cool!
School is so cool!

7 Listen.

Culture Special

Children at an English school

8 **Speak.**

7 CD 1/8

9 Listen and fill in the numbers.

2	Wash your face.	1	Have a glass of milk.
8	Put your rubber in your pencil case.	6	Get your scissors.
7	Get out of bed.	4	Put on your T-shirt.
5	Put your books in your schoolbag.	3	Check your watch.

10 Match.

4 
7 
8 
2 
6 
3 
1 
5 

11 Write the words.

three ten ~~eight~~ one five nine six two seven four

red blue white ~~yellow~~ green black orange pink brown grey

8	eight	yellow
4	for	grenn
1	one	brown
9	nine	grey
5	five	pink
10	ten	white
3	three	blue
2	two	orange
7	seven	black
6	six	red

Unit 2

Pets

1 Listen and point.

2 Test your partner.

1 CD 1/10

3 Listen and tick (✓).

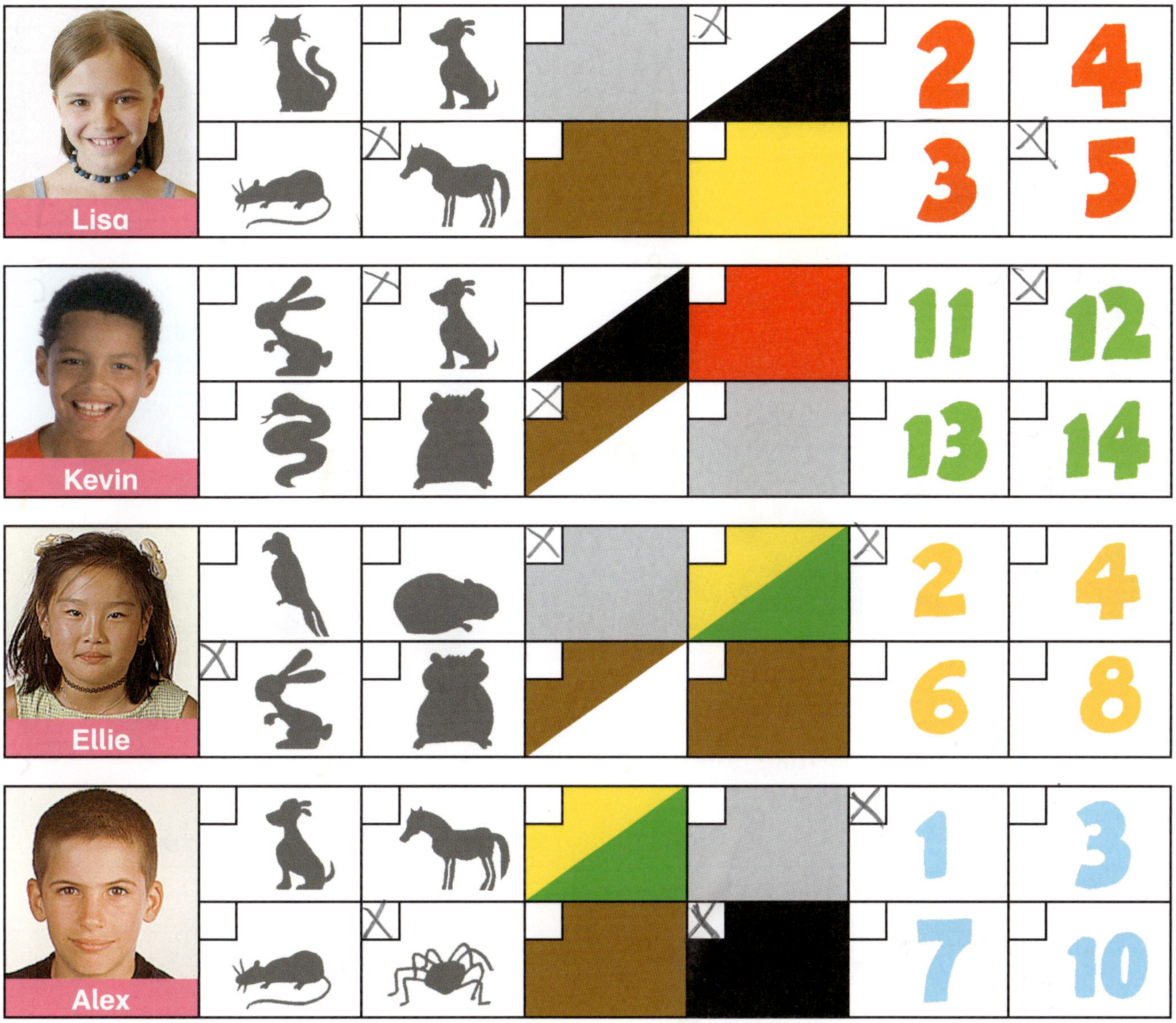

4 Talk about the children's pets.

3 CD 1/11

5 Listen and complete.

hamster three brown

6 Ask five classmates. Take notes.

Name	Animal	Colour	How old?
Natalie	hamster	brown	3
David	/	/	/

7 Tell the class.

5 CD 1/12

8 Watch the story. Read and write the numbers.

Pets

1. We want a pet.
2. Take the goldfish back to the shop.
3. I've got an idea.
4. Pets are great!

9 Listen. Sing the song.

Mice, mice, mice

Mice, mice, mice,
I like their little ears.

Mice, mice, mice,
I like their little feet.

Mice, mice, mice,
I like their little teeth.
Yes, little mice are really nice!

My mum hates mice,
my dad hates mice,
but I think mice are really nice.

I give them cheese,
I give them rice.
Yes, mice are really nice!

10 Read. Write your own text.

My text

I haven't got a pet.
My grandma has a budgie.
The budgie's name is Jimmy.
It's blue, yellow and green.
Lucy

My text

I've got a cat and a dog.
My cat is three and
my dog is four years old.
The cat's name is Socks.
The dog's name is Buddy.
Paul

9 CD 1/13–14

11  **Do the hedgehog quiz. Read the questions and circle the correct answer/picture. Then listen and check.**

1 What do hedgehogs eat?

2 What do they do in winter?

3 When do they eat?

4 How long do they live?

1–2 years | 4–5 years | 11–12 years

5 How many spikes have they got?

200 | 500 | 800

6 What are they scared of?

7 What do they do when there is danger?

6–7 Very good!

3–5 Good!

1–2 Try again!

Unit 3

I'm scared

Note
not scared
scared

1 Listen and draw the faces or .

2 Tell the class.

1 CD 1/16

3 Listen and tick (✔).

	Susan	Sam	Jessica and Grace	Oliver and Chris
	☐	☐	☐	☐
	☐	☐	☐	☐
	☐	☐	☐	☐
	☐	☐	☐	☐
	☐	☐	☐	☐
	☐	☐	☐	☐
	☐	☐	☐	☐
	☐	☐	☐	☐

4 Ask a partner.

5 Watch the story. Then listen and write.

The goat

check goat What a Go away!

Help! Help! | Thank you! | Go away! | please

6 Listen and mime. Then listen and point.

A monster is looking at you

7 Listen and fill in the numbers.

8 Listen and speak.

9 Write your own rhyme and draw a picture.

a croc in my sock

a bee on my knee

a rat on my hat

a bear on my chair

a mouse in my house

a bird in my shirt

a fly in my eye

a snake in my cake

10 Read. Write your own text.

My text

I'm scared of spiders and snakes.
I'm not scared of dogs.
I like dogs.
But my dad is scared of dogs.

8 CD 1/21

Show what you can do

1 **Read and fill in the numbers.**

1 

2 

3 

4 

5 

6 

7 

8 

9 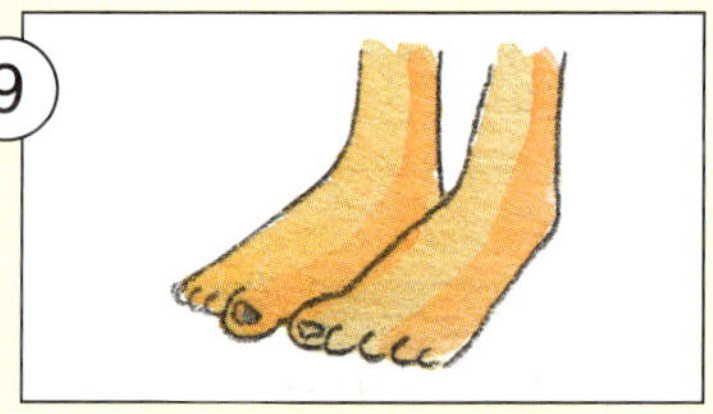

10 

11 

12 

(8) scared	(1) bird	(3) goat
(4) he	(6) shirt	(11) they
(2) eye	(10) eat	(5) snake
(12) teeth	(7) she	(9) feet

2 Match. Fill in the numbers.

1	Are you scared of snakes?	5	He's three.
2	What's your name?	8	There's a dog in our garden.
3	Have you got a pet?	7	It's green.
4	Is Lauren scared of ghosts?	3	Yes, a cat.
5	How old is your dog?	4	No, she isn't.
6	What's your telephone number?	1	No, I'm not.
7	What colour is your pencil case?	2	I'm Robert.
8	What's that?	6	834602.

3 Write the missing words.

~~Put on~~ ~~Wash~~ ~~Get out~~ ~~Check~~ ~~Put~~ Have ~~Stop~~

Put on your book in your schoolbag.

Stop eating my toast!

Get out of bed.

Check your watch.

Wash your face.

Put on your jeans.

Have a glass of milk.

Unit 4

Weather

1 Listen. What are the animals' names? Say the rhyme.

Scott	Jane	Peter	Stuart	Joe

2 Listen and point.

spring

summer

autumn

winter

1 CD 1/22 2 CD 1/23

3 Listen and mime. Then listen and point.

What's the weather like?

4 Listen and fill in the numbers.

3 CD 1/24 4 CD 1/25

5 Watch the story. Then listen and write.

Six hungry caterpillars

hungry Monday Thursday Tuesday

Mr Smith has a beautiful garden.

In the garden there are six hungry caterpillars.

On Monday they eat the leaves of the apple tree.

On Tuesday they eat the leaves of the pear tree.

On Wednesday they eat the leaves of the plum tree.

On Thusday they eat the leaves of the peach tree.

 5 CD 1/26

Friday butterflies shop Saturday

6 Listen. Do the chant.

Cold and hot

It's cold outside.
Put on your jacket.
It's cold outside.
Put on your hat.
It's cold outside.
Put on your mittens.
OK, let's go.

Let's go inside.
OK, let's go.
It's hot in here.
Take off your mittens.
It's hot in here.
Take off your hat.
It's hot in here.
Take off your jacket.
Ah, that's better.

7 **Make a thermometer.**

You need:

- a transparent straw
- a small bottle with cold water
- a bowl
- modelling clay
- hot water

1 Put the straw in the bottle.

2 Put the modelling clay around it to hold it in place.

3 Put hot water into a bowl.

4 Put the bottle into the bowl.

Think and guess.
What happens?

Then do the experiment.

?

The water in the straw rises.
It's a thermometer.

Unit 5

What's the time?

1 Watch the story. Then listen and write.

Midnight on the farm

twelve | You're | asleep | midnight | What

1 CD 1/30

~~Playing~~ ~~Stop!~~ ~~What's~~ ~~Head~~ ~~Where~~

2 Listen and point.

cat

bat

dog

frog

fox

ox

mouse

louse

3 Listen. Do the chant.

4 Write your own chant. Draw a picture.

5 **Watch the story. Read and write the numbers.**

Going to a party

1 Lots of time to do my hair.
2 Lots of time to clean my shoes.
3 Lots of time to have a snack.
4 Lots of time to iron my shirt.

6  Listen. Find Tina, Christine and Sally. Write their names.

1

It's ________________ .

2

It's ________________ .

3

It's ________________ .

7 Read. Write your own text.

My text

I get up at quarter past six.
I have breakfast at half past six.
I go to school at seven.
I come home at half past twelve.
I go to bed at half past eight.

 6 CD 1/35

8 **Test your partner. What can he/she do in a minute?**

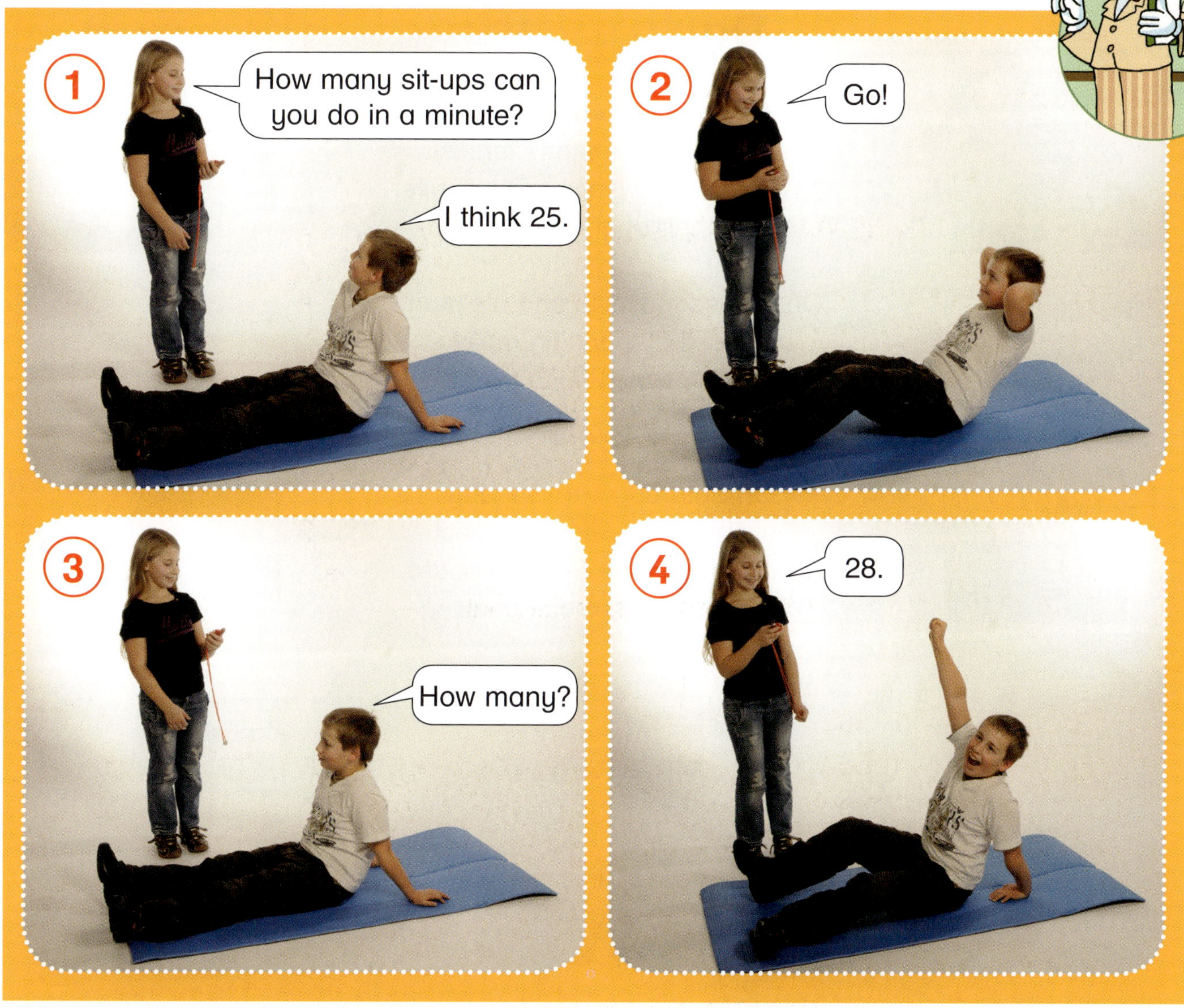

Free time

1 **Listen. Say the chant. Do the actions.**

(1)

(2)

David's week

On Monday David rides his horse,
on Tuesday he plays tennis.
On Wednesday Dave and Jennifer
sail their boat to Venice.

On Thursday David and his mum
go to the shopping mall.
On Friday David rides his bike,
and he plays volleyball.

On Saturday and Sunday
Dave's at the swimming pool.
He dives from the 5-metre board.
Hey! That is really cool!

(7)

(6)

(3)

(4)

(5)

2 **Read, look and say.**

 1 CD 2/1–3

3 What can the children do? Listen and tick (✓). Then talk about the children.

Claire

ride a horse	✓
sail a boat	✗
skate	✓

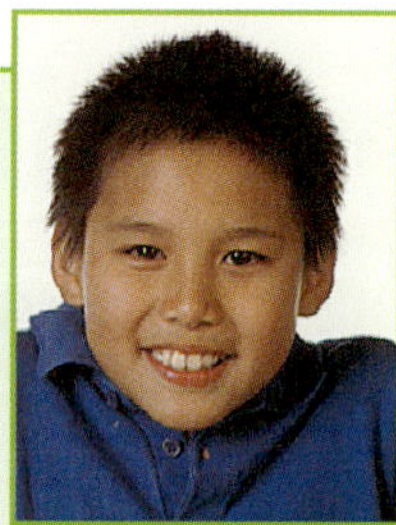

Robert

swim	✓
play tennis	✗
ski	✓

Abigail

swim	✓
ice-skate	✓
play football	✓

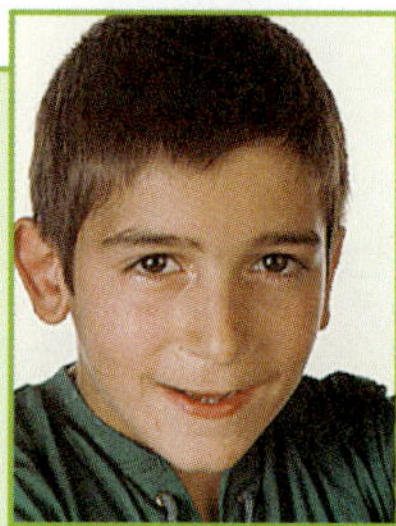

James

ride a horse	✗
sail a boat	✓
dance	✗

4 Talk in class.

5 Listen. Sing the song.

Busy Lizzy

Her name is Lizzy,
and she's so busy.
She's got so many
things to do.

She feeds the squirrels in the park,
she plays the saxophone.
She rides her bike around the town
and then she dances with a clown.

Her name is …

She goes sailing every day,
and she plays volleyball.
She cooks spaghetti for her friends,
her busy day just never ends.

Her name is …

6 Read and tick *True* or *False* (✔).

	True	False
Lizzy feeds the ducks in the park.		X
She plays the saxophone.	X	
Lizzy dances with a sheriff.		X

	True	False
She plays volleyball.	X	
She goes shopping every day.		X
Lizzy cooks fish and chips for her friends.		X

5 CD 2/5–6

7 Listen and mime. Then listen and point.

The bike trip

8 Listen and fill in the numbers.

9 Watch the story. Read and write the numbers.

A sport for Mr Matt

1. Sure. Go ahead.
2. I'll get you.
3. Yes. Can I join in?
4. Dad, you watch too much TV.

10 Look and write. Then create your own text about Ronnie.

skate ski ride a bike cook spaghetti

Ronnie can't ski.

He can't ride a bike.

He can't skate.

But he can cook spaghetti.

11 Read. Write your own text.

My text

I can sail a boat.
I'm good at it.
I can skate and ride
a unicycle.
I can't play tennis.

My text

My best friend is Oliver.
He is nine.
He plays football a lot.
He is very good at it.

Units **4–6**

Show what you can do

1 **Read and fill in the numbers.**

1 

2 

3 

4 

5 

6 

7 

8 

9 

10 

11 

12 

(3) squirrel
(7) hot
(9) leaves

(5) hungry
(10) fog
(11) jacket

(12) spring
(8) strawberry
(1) cold

(4) frog
(6) sun
(2) rain

2 Look and write.

It's quarter to four. It's half past four. It's quarter past four. It's four o'clock.

It's four o'clock. ✓

It's half past four. ✓

It's quarter past four. ✓

It's quarter to four. ✓

3 Match and write.

swim dive go skating play football ride a horse sail a boat

ride a horse

sail a boat

go skating

dive

play football

swim

At home

1 Listen and point.

1 CD 2/9

2 Play the game.

3 Look at the picture on page 42. Ask and answer.

Where are Tom's socks?
Where's his cap?
Where are his jeans?
Where's his schoolbag?

Where are Kate's trainers?
Where's her T-shirt?
Where's her pullover?
Where's her umbrella?

4 Watch the story. Then listen and write.

The hats in the attic

scared Who princess attic What

 4 CD 2/10

shoe give it Take marry can't

5 Make a desk, a chair, a bed and a wardrobe.
Listen to Simon and put the things in his room.

6 Listen. Sing the song.

The racoon in my room

There's a racoon,
a little racoon,
a little racoon
in my room, oh yes!

He's drinking my milk
and he's eating my bread,
he's breaking my toys
and he's using my bed.

Please, Mum, don't come in.
There's a mess in my room.
I think my racoon
won't leave before June.

Don't tell anybody
my little racoon
is just an excuse
for the mess in my room.

7 Read. Write your own text.

My room

In my room there's a nice bed.
The desk is in front of the window.
Next to the desk there's a big wardrobe.
There are three posters in my room.
On the posters there are horses.

6 CD 2/12–13

Unit 8

Feelings

1 **Listen and point.**

happy | sad | scared | tired | angry

2 **Listen and tick (✔). Say.**

1 Thirteen monkeys are dancing on the bed.					
2 Thirteen monkeys are dancing on the bed.					
3 Thirteen monkeys are dancing on the bed.					
4 Thirteen monkeys are dancing on the bed.					
5 Thirteen monkeys are dancing on the bed.					

3 **Crazy sentences. Work with a partner.**

Emily, kiss the apple tree!

There's a fox with yellow socks.

Put on your football.

There's a pink hippo in our garden.

 1 CD 2/14 **2** CD 2/15

4 **Play the game with a partner.**

Tell me about Lisa.

No, sorry. She's happy.

What about Tom?

That's right.

I think she's angry.

I think he's sad.

5 **Listen to the dialogues.**

Dialogue 1:

Girl: Are you angry?
Boy: No, I'm not.
Girl: What's the problem?
Boy: I'm hungry.

Dialogue 2:

Boy: Are you sad?
Girl: Yes, I am.
Boy: What's the problem?
Girl: My dog's ill.

6 **Work in pairs. Change the dialogues. Act them out.**

7 Watch the story. Then listen and write.

Snow White

Here you are. | very angry | the best singer | Where

 7 CD 2/17

again must very happy a big star

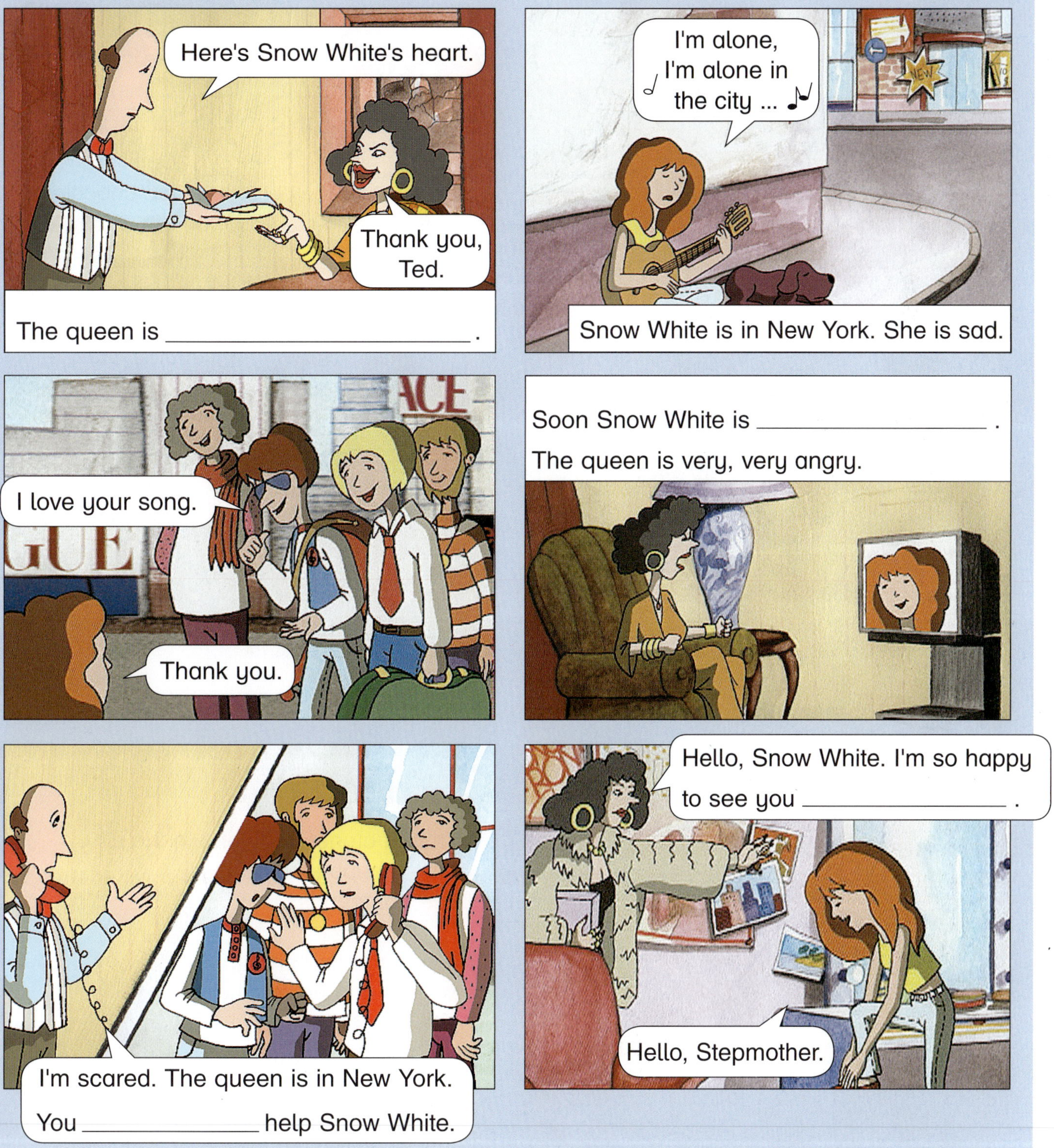

8 Listen. Sing the song.

Friends

I'm not alone, not alone in the city.
I'm so happy, so happy
I've got friends.

We laugh and shout,
we run around and hop.
We sing and dance,
we never, never stop.

I'm not alone, not alone in the city.
I'm so happy, so happy
I've got friends.

8 CD 2/18–19

9 Listen and mime. Then listen and point.

The football

10 Listen and fill in the numbers.

11 Listen and point.

tired

angry

greedy

scared

hungry

bored

thirsty

nervous

12 Listen. Do the chant.

A happy frog

A happy frog,
a hungry dog,
a sad fox,
a tired ox,
an angry bat,
and a thirsty cat
are having a chat
just like that.

13 Write your own chant. Draw a picture.

14 **Expressions. Read the questions and circle the correct picture.**

1 Who is happy?

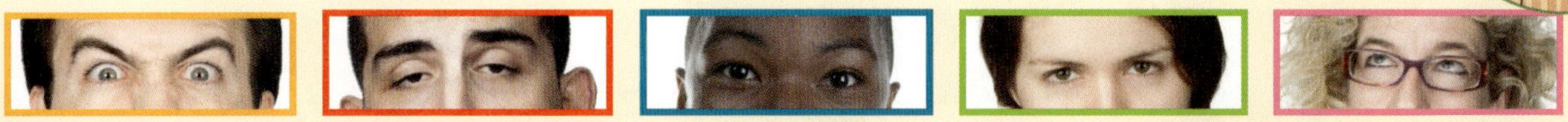

2 Who is sad?

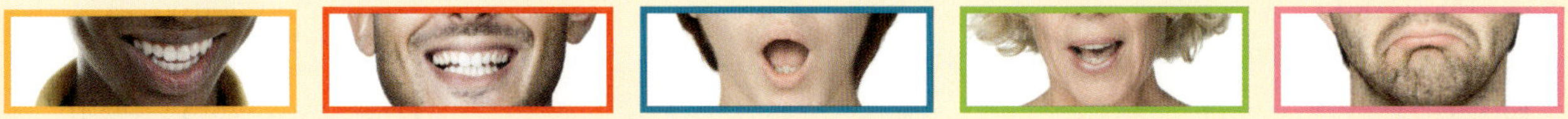

3 Who is scared?

4 Who is angry?

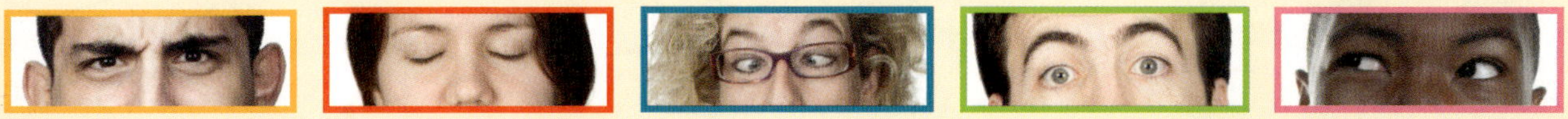

5 Who is tired?

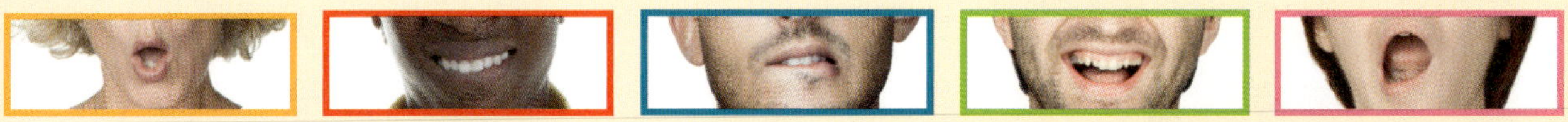

Unit 9

Shopping

1 Listen. Sing the song.

1 CD 2/26–27

Culture Special

2 Listen and point.

British money

3 **How much money have they got? Read and write.**

1. Ben has got £5. He buys a book for £2.50.
How much has he got now? £ ______________

2. Laura has got £8. She buys scissors for 90p.
How much has she got now? £ ______________

3. Paul has got £11. He buys stickers for £4.
How much has he got now? £ ______________

4. Bill has got £6. He buys a pen for 50p and
a magazine for £1.50. How much has he got now? £ ______________

5. Caroline has got £15. She buys a DVD for £7
and sweets for 50p. How much has she got now? £ ______________

6. Michelle has got £9.90. She buys a CD for £4.50.
How much has she got now? £ ______________

4 Listen and point.

vegetables

fruit

5 Listen and read. Then change and act out.

Girl: Good morning.

Shopkeeper: Good morning. Can I help you?

Girl: 3 green peppers and a kilo of tomatoes, please.

Shopkeeper: That's £2.65.

Girl: Here you are.

Shopkeeper: Thank you.

Girl: Goodbye.

Shopkeeper: Bye-bye.

4 CD 2/29 5 CD 2/30

6 Watch the story. Read and write.

Going shopping

It's very good! I forgot the fish.
Sorry, Dad! We're busy. Can you go shopping?

7 Listen and mime. Then listen and point.

No money, no sweets

8 Listen and fill in the numbers.

9 Listen and read. Then speak.

Tom:	Two ice creams, please.
Shopkeeper:	What flavours?
Emma:	For me vanilla and chocolate, please.
Tom:	And for me strawberry and yoghurt, please.
Shopkeeper:	OK. Here you are.
Tom:	How much is it?
Shopkeeper:	£2.
Emma:	Here you are.
Shopkeeper:	Thank you.
Tom and Emma:	Goodbye.

10 Change the dialogue and act it out.

11 Read. Write your own text.

My text

I often go shopping for my mum.
I buy fruit and vegetables.
I buy tomatoes, yoghurt and milk.

Show what you can do

1 **Write the answers.**

① Where are the jeans?

They are ______________________________.

② Where's the book?

It's ______________________________.

③ Where are the socks?

______________________________.

④ Where are the trainers?

______________________________.

⑤ Where's the cat?

______________________________.

⑥ Where's the ball?

______________________________.

2 **Put the dialogue in the correct order. Write the numbers.**

◯ No, I'm not.

◯ I'm sad. My dog is ill.

◯ Are you tired?

◯ What's the problem?

3 **Read and write.**

is	looks	please	white	Here	are

Excuse me.

Yes, please.

How much ____________ the jeans?

They're £31.

Ah, this pink and ____________ T-shirt

____________ great.

How much ____________ it?

£6.

OK. The jeans and the T-shirt,

____________.

That's £37.

____________ you are.

Thank you.

Christmas

1 Listen and read.

Culture Special

Christmas in Britain and Australia

Hi, I'm Christina from Cambridge. This is our Christmas.

On Christmas Day we have Christmas dinner. Here you see my brother Pete, my grandma and grandpa, and my mum and dad.

This is a Christmas cracker.

This is my brother Mike. He is opening his presents on Christmas Day.

Hi, I'm Mark from Sydney.

On Christmas Day we often have a party on the beach. These are my parents and their friends.

On Christmas Eve we hang up our Christmas stockings.

1 CD 2/34

Word list

A

airport	**Flughafen**
alone	**alleine**
angry (PW2)	**wütend**
apple (PW1)	**Apfel**
at home	**zu Hause**
attic	**Dachboden**
autumn	**Herbst**

B

banana	**Banane**
bat	**Fledermaus**
bathroom (PW2)	**Badezimmer**
bear	**Bär**
beautiful	**wunderschön**
bed (PW1)	**Bett**
bedroom	**Schlafzimmer**
behind	**hinter**
best friend	**bester** Freund
better	**besser**
bike (trip)	**Rad(ausflug)**
bird	**Vogel**
black (PW1)	**schwarz**
board	**Tafel**
book	**Buch**
have **breakfast** (PW1)	**frühstücken**
brown (PW1)	**braun**
budgie	**Wellensittich**
busy (PW2)	**beschäftigt**
butterfly (PW1)	**Schmetterling**
buy	**kaufen**

C

cake (PW1)	**Kuchen/Torte**
can (PW1)	**können**
Can I help you?	**Kann ich dir/ Ihnen helfen?**
(play) **cards**	**Karten** (spielen)
carrot (PW2)	**Karotte**
cat (PW1)	**Katze**
caterpillar	**Raupe**
chair (PW1)	**Stuhl**
cheese (PW1)	**Käse**
child, children (PW2)	**Kind, Kinder**
chocolate (PW1)	**Schokolade**
Christmas (PW1)	**Weihnachten**
clean	**putzen**
It's … o'**clock.**	**Es ist … Uhr.**
close (the door)	(die Türe) **schließen**
clothes (PW2)	**Kleidung**
cold (PW1)	**kalt**
colour	**Farbe**
come home	**nach Hause kommen**
cook spaghetti	**Spaghetti kochen**
cool (PW1)	**cool/toll;** auch: **kühl**
crazy (PW2)	**verrückt**
crocodile	**Krokodil**
cucumber	**Gurke**

D

dance (PW2)	**tanzen**
danger	**Gefahr**
desk	**Schreibtisch**
dinner	**Abendessen**
dive (PW2)	**einen Kopfsprung ins Wasser machen**
dog (PW1)	**Hund**

E

eat (PW1)	**essen**
eighty	**achtzig**
every day	**jeden Tag**
eye (PW1)	**Auge**

F

face (PW1)	**Gesicht**
farmer	**Bauer**
feed squirrels	Eichhörnchen **füttern**
fifty	**fünfzig**
fit	**passen**
(gold)**fish**	(Gold)**Fisch**
flavour	**Geschmack**
fly away	**wegfliegen**
fly	hier: **Fliege**
fog	**Nebel**
(play) **football**	**Fußball** (spielen)
forty	**vierzig**
fox (PW2)	**Fuchs**
Friday	**Freitag**
frog (PW1)	**Frosch**
fruit (PW1)	**Obst**

G

garden (PW2)	**Garten**
get up	**aufstehen**
ghost	**Geist**

give (PW1)	**geben**
have a **glass of milk**	ein **Glas Milch** trinken
glue	**Klebstoff**
go (PW1)	**gehen**
goat	**Ziege**
good idea	**gute Idee**
Good morning!	**Guten Morgen!**
Goodbye!	**Auf Wiedersehen!**
grandma (PW2)	**Großmutter, Oma**
great (PW2)	**großartig**
green (PW1)	**grün**
green/red peppers	**grüne/rote Paprika**
grey (PW1)	**grau**
guinea pig	**Meerschweinchen**

H

half past three	**halb** vier Uhr
hall	**Vorzimmer**
hamster	**Hamster**
happy (PW2)	**glücklich**
hat (PW2)	**Hut**
Have fun!	**Viel Spaß!**
have/has got (PW1)	**haben**
heart	**Herz**
hedgehog	**Igel**
help (PW1)	**helfen, Hilfe**
hippo (PW1)	**Nilpferd**
hot (PW2)	**heiß**
house (PW2)	**Haus**
how (PW1)	**wie**
How much is/are...?	**Wieviel kostet ...?**
(a) **hundred**	**hundert**
hungry (PW1)	**hungrig**
hurry up (PW2)	**sich beeilen**

I

I'm ... (PW1)	**Ich bin/heiße ...**
ice cream (PW1)	**Eis**
ice-skate	**eislaufen**
ill	**krank**
in front of	**vor**
in (PW1)	**in**
insect	**Insekt**
inside	**drinnen**
iron my **shirt**	mein **Hemd bügeln**
is (PW1)	**ist**
it (PW1)	**es**

J

jacket (PW2)	**Jacke**

K

kiss	**küssen**
kitchen (PW1)	**Küche**
knee (PW1)	**Knie**

L

laugh	**lachen**
leaf/leaves	**Blatt/Blätter**
lemon	**Zitrone**
like (PW1)	**hier: mögen**
live (PW2)	**leben**
living room	**Wohnzimmer**
louse	**Laus**

M

marry	**heiraten**
mess	**Unordnung**
mice (pl.) (PW1)	**Mäuse**
midnight	**Mitternacht**
mirror	**Spiegel**
mittens	**Fäustlinge/ Handschuhe**
Monday	**Montag**
money	**Geld**
monster	**Monster**
month	**Monat**
mouse (PW1)	**Maus**
must	**müssen**

N

next (to)	**neben**
ninety	**neunzig**
no	**nein**

O

on	**auf**
onion (PW2)	**Zwiebel**
orange	**Orange**
outside (PW1)	**draußen**
ox	**Ochse**

P

peach	**Pfirsich**
pear (PW1)	**Birne**
pen	**Stift**
pencil case (PW1)	**Federpennal**
pencil (PW1)	**Bleistift**
pet (PW1)	**Haustier**
piggy bank	**Sparschwein**
play (PW1)	**spielen; Theaterstück**
please	**bitte**
plum	**Zwetschke**
pony	**Pony**
potato (PW2)	**Kartoffel**
present (PW1)	**Geschenk**
put on (PW1)	**anziehen**

Q

a **quarter to** nine	**viertel vor** neun
a **quarter past** nine	**viertel nach** neun
queen	**Königin**

R

rabbit (PW1)	**Kaninchen**
racoon	**Waschbär**
rain (PW1)	**Regen**
rat	**Ratte**
raven	**Rabe**
red (PW1)	**rot**
ride a bike	**radfahren**
ride a horse	**reiten**
room (PW2)	**Zimmer**
rubber	**Radiergummi**
ruler	**Lineal**
run (PW1)	**laufen, rennen**

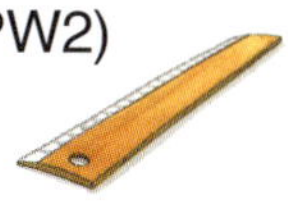

S

sad	**traurig**
sail a boat (PW2)	**segeln**
Saturday (PW2)	**Samstag**
(play) **the saxophone**	**Saxophon** (spielen)
We are scared of …	**Wir fürchten uns vor …**
school (PW1)	**Schule**
schoolbag	**Schultasche**
scissors (PW1)	**Schere**
seventy	**siebzig**
shirt	**Hemd**
go **shopping**	**einkaufen gehen**
shopping mall	**Einkaufszentrum**
shout	**rufen, schreien**
sing a song (PW1)	**ein Lied singen**
singer	**Sänger/in**
sixty	**sechzig**
go **skating**	**inline skaten**
skeleton	**Skelett**
ski	**Schi fahren**
smile	**lächeln**
snow (PW1)	**Schnee**
sock (PW2)	**Socke**
spider (PW1)	**Spinne**
spike	**Stachel**
spring	**Frühling**
stairs	**Stiege, Treppe**
stepmother	**Stiefmutter**
strawberry	**Erdbeere**
stupid	**dumm**
summer	**Sommer**
sun (PW1)	**Sonne**
Sunday	**Sonntag**
sweets	**Süßigkeiten**
swim (PW2)	**schwimmen**

T

telephone number	**Telefonnummer**
ten	**zehn**
(play) **tennis**	**Tennis** (spielen)
thirsty (PW1)	**durstig**
thirty	**dreißig**
Thursday	**Donnerstag**
tired	**müde**
tomato (PW2)	**Tomate**
tortoise	**Landschildkröte**
tree (PW2)	**Baum**
trip over something	**über etwas stolpern**
Tuesday	**Dienstag**
twenty	**zwanzig**

U

under	**unter**
umbrella	**Regenschirm**

V

vanilla	**Vanille**
vegetables (PW2)	**Gemüse**
very (PW1)	**sehr**
(play) **volleyball**	**Volleyball** (spielen)

W

wake up	**aufwachen**
walk	**gehen**
want	**wollen**
wardrobe	**Schrank**
wash	**waschen**
watch TV (=television)	**fernsehen**
watch	**Armbanduhr**
Wednesday	**Mittwoch**
week (PW1)	**Woche**
What's the problem?	**Was ist los?**
What's the time?	**Wie spät ist es?**
What's your name?	**Wie heißt du?**

When?	**Wann?**
Where is/are ...? (PW1)	**Wo ist/sind ...?**
white	**weiß**
window	**Fenster**
winter (PW1)	**Winter**
witch(es)	**Hexe(n)**

Y

year (PW2)	**Jahr**
yellow (PW1)	**gelb**
you (PW1)	**du/Sie**
yes	**ja**
yoghurt	**Jogurt**

PLAYWAY

Elterninformation

Liebe Eltern, so funktioniert Englischlernen mit *PLAYWAY*

◆ Ihr Kind lernt
- die Bedeutung und Schreibweise englischer Wörter mit Hilfe von ***Picture Cards*** und ***Word Cards***.
- die Aussprache neuer Wörter mit Hilfe von Liedern und Reimen von einer **Audio-CD**.
- lustige Sketches und Geschichten durch Videosequenzen auf **DVD** zu verstehen.
- einfache Dialoge auf Englisch zu führen.

ISBN 978-3-85061-635-5
Preis: € 39,90

Spaß am Nachmittag oder Wochenende gibt es bei PLAYWAY natürlich auch.

PLAYWAY – Die CD-ROM für zu Hause

Mit der interaktiven und multimedialen Englisch-Training-Software geht's auf in die virtuelle Welt von Max und seinen Freunden, die alle in einer ganz besonderen Straße im *PLAYWAY*-Land leben: der Lern- und Spielstraße.
Hier gibt es die unterschiedlichsten Stationen, an denen die Kinder ihre Englischkenntnisse auf den Prüfstand stellen können. Klar, dass Max immer hilft, wenn's mal klemmt.

Die CD-ROM bietet:
- mehr als 20 Stunden Übungsmaterial
- 15 Übungstypen mit 25 Varianten
- ca. 45 Minuten voll animierte *Cartoons*
- Karaoke Funktion für *Songs* und *Chants*
- ein mitwachsendes *Dictionary*
- einen kapitelweisen Aufbau für einen einfachen Zugriff.

Systemvoraussetzungen:
Betriebssysteme: Windows 2000, XP, Vista, Win7; Prozessor: Pentium/Celeron/Athlon/Thunderbird, mind. 1000 MHz; Arbeitsspeicher: Unter Win 2000, Win XP: mind. 256 MB, Vista, Win7: 1024 MB Freier Speicherplatz auf der Festplatte: mind. 800 MB; CD-ROM Laufwerk/Soundkarte; Grafikkarte: mind. 16 Bit Farbe (High Color)

Infos und Prospekte direkt bei

HELBLING
Verlagsgesellschaft m.b.H.
Kaplanstraße 9
Postfach 12
A-6063 Rum
Tel. 0512/262333-0
Fax 0512/262333-111

E-Mail:
office@helbling.co.at

Homepage:
www.helbling.at

Bestellkarte für *Kinder*, Eltern und Lehrer!

Stück	Titel		Preis
		**PLAYWAY 3 CD-ROM** 978-3-85061-635-5 Multimediales Englisch-Training mit Max CD-ROM mit umfangreichem Booklet	**€ 39,90**

Datum

Unterschrift (Bei minderjährigen der Erziehungsberechtigte)

Die Lieferung erfolgt auf Rechnung zuzüglich Portokosten. Unverbindliche Preisempfehlung.
Preise freibleibend, Stand 1.11.2010; Änderungen vorbehalten.

Helbling

PLAYWAY

Spielerisch Lernen – mit System

EINFACH ZU BESTELLEN!
Die beiliegende Bestellkarte zum Ausschneiden einfach in einer Buchhandlung abgeben oder an folgende Adresse senden:

→ *www.helbling.at*

HELBLING Verlagsgesellschaft m.b.H.
A-6063 RUM · Kaplanstraße 9 · Postfach 12
Tel. 0512/262333-0 · Fax 0512/262333-111

Sie können auch via Internet bestellen.

Unsere E-Mail-Adresse lautet:
office@helbling.co.at

oder Sie besuchen unsere Homepage.
Hier finden Sie, neben unserem Bestellservice und der umfangreichen Produktinfo, auch viele interessante Anregungen und Tipps für Eltern und Kids:

www.helbling.at

Absender:
(Bitte in Blockschrift!)

E-Mail:

Vorname Familienname

Straße

Postleitzahl Ort

Schule (Name und Ort)

Antwort

An

HELBLING
Verlagsgesellschaft m.b.H.

Kaplanstraße 9 · Postfach 12
A-6063 RUM

Helbling